Message
on a Rocket

Written by Elizabeth Strauss
Illustrated by Eric Strauss

sundance

One day, an alien
found a message
from a boy named
Tyler.

The message was
seven pages long.

The first page said,
"You are invited
to my sleepover."

The second page said,
"Go to the
Milky Way Galaxy."

A picture showed
how the galaxy looks
from the top
and from the sides.

First, go to the Milky Way Galaxy. It looks like this from the top:

Our solar system is about here

It looks like this from the side:

The third page showed
our solar system.

The message said to find
the third planet
from the Sun.

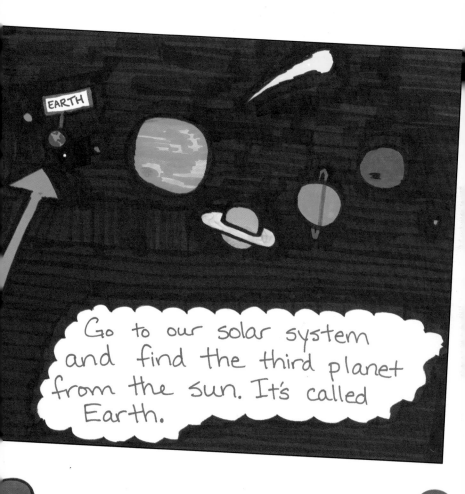

Go to our solar system and find the third planet from the sun. It's called Earth.

The fourth page showed our planet, Earth.

The message said to find the side of Earth that has North America.

The fifth page showed
North America. It also
showed a gas station.

The message said
how to find the town
where Tyler lives.

The sixth page showed a
street map of Tyler's town.

The message said
how to find Tyler's house.

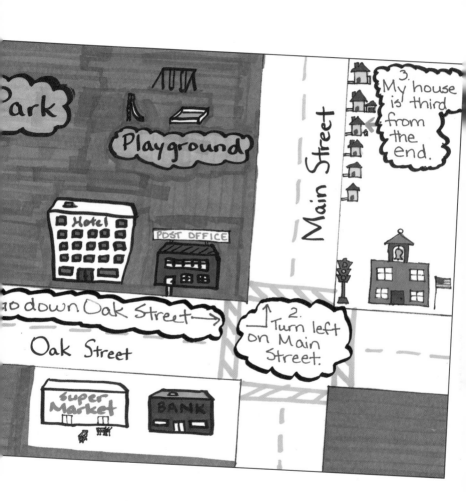

The seventh page showed the outside and the inside of Tyler's house.

The message said how to find Tyler's bedroom.

This is what my house looks like.

So, the alien took the message to his mother to ask if he could go.

What do you think she said?